For
Chris
With love,
Sandy
April 1991

Woman
to
Woman

Copyright 1995 © Great Quotations Publishing Company

All rights reserved. No part of this work may be reproduced
or transmitted in any form or by any means, electronic or
mechanical, including photocopying, recording or by any
information storage and retrieval system, without permission
in writing from the publisher.

ISBN 1-56245-194-4

Original Art by Anne Kilham of Rockport, Maine

Published in the United States by
Great Quotations Publishing Company
1967 Quincy Court
Glendale Heights, IL 60139

Printed in Hong Kong

*Dedicated to all women,
past, present & future.*

The Serpent beguiled me, and I did eat.

Eve (Genesis, 3:13)

Watch out, my dear, there's a scorpion under every stone.

Praxilla (451 BC)

*Leave the fishing-rod,
Great General, to us sovereigns
of Pharaohs and Canopus.
Your game is cities and kings
and continents.*

Cleopatra VII (69 BC-AD 30)

*I am yours, you are mine.
Of this we are
certain.
You are lodged
in my heart,
the small key
is lost.
You must stay there
forever.*

Frau Ava (?-1127)

Two yards of veil won't make any woman a lady; nor a hat make any head worthy of command.

Padeshah Khatun (14th Century)

I have heard say the executioner is very good, and I have a little neck.

Anne Boleyn (1507-1536)

Reader, I have oft been told,
Verses that speak not Love are cold.

Anna Hume (fl. 1644)

❦

The key to my locked spirit is your laughing mouth.

Nur Jahan (?-1946)

*But, lady, as women what wisdom may be ours if not the philosophies of the kitchen? Leonardo spoke well when he said: how well one may philosophize when preparing dinner.
And I often say, when observing these trivial details: had Aristotle prepared victuals, he would have written more.*

Juanna Ines de la Cruz (1651-1695)

Women are from their very infancy debar'd those advantages of education with the want of which they are afterwards reproached, and nursed up in those vices with which will hereafter be upbraided them. So partial are Men as to expect bricks when they afford no straw.

Mary Astell (1666-1731)

It is a sin to be content with a little knowledge.

Anne Baynard (1672-1697)

We women as naturally love scandal, as you men do debauchery; and we can no more keep up conversation without one, than you can live an age without t'other.

Mary Davys (1674-1732)

A woman, till five-and-thirty, is only looked upon as a raw girl, and can possibly make no noise in the world till about forty.

Mary Wortley Montagu (1689-1762)

I will not be cheated—nor will I employ long years of repentance for moments of joy.

Ibid

...it is now eleven years since I have seen my figure in a glass, and the last reflection I saw there was so disagreeable, that I resolved to spare myself the mortification in the future.

Mary Wortley Montagu (1689-1762)

The knowledge of numbers is one of the chief distinctions between us and the brutes.

Ibid

*Why should marriage bring
only tears?
All I wanted was a man
With a single heart,
And we would stay together
As our hair turned white,
Not somebody always after
wriggling fish
With his big bamboo rod.*

        Chuo Wen-Chun (179-117 BC)

Sisters beware of all pride, vain ambition; envy, greed, and of taking part in the cares and busy ways of the world.

Clare of Assisi (1193-1253)

*Love appears every day for one who offers love,
That wisdom is enough.*

Hadewijch (fl. 1235-1265)

Make two homes for thyself, my daughter. One actual home and another spiritual home, which thou art to carry with thee always.

Catherine of Siena (1347-1380)

Messire, I am but a poor village girl; I cannot ride on horseback nor lead men to battle.

Joan of Arc (1412-1431)

If it were customary to send little girls to school and to teach them the same subjects as are taught to boys, they would learn just as fully and would understand the subtleties of all arts and sciences. Indeed, maybe they would understand them better... for just as women's bodies are softer than men's so their understanding is sharper.

Christine de Pisan (1363-1430)

I, a woman, have dropped the symbols of my sex.
Yarn, shuttle, basket, thread.

Olimpia Morata (1526-1555)

All my possessions for a moment of time.

Elizabeth I of England (1533-1603)

*I have prayed for thee,
that thou mightest be fortunate
in two hours of thy life time:
in the hour of thy marriage,
and at the hour of thy death.*

Elizabeth Grymeston (1563-1603)

When anything is written by a woman, that men cannot deny their approbation to, they are sure to rob us of the glory of it, by concluding 'tis not her own; or at least, that she had some assistance, which has been said in many instances to my knowledge unjustly.

Catherine Cockburn (1679-1749)

Here and in the other world happiness comes to a person, not a gender.

Honnamma (1665-1699)

I think that pleasures should be enjoyed with great sobriety and moderation.

Rosalba Carriera (1675-1757)

Marriage is a lottery in which men stake their liberty and women their happiness.

Renee de Chateauneuf Rieux (1550-1587)

Let no one ever say that marriages are made in Heaven; the gods would not commit so great an injustice!

Marguerite of Valois (1553-1616)

You can come into no company of ladies and or gentlemen, where you shall not hear an open and vehement exclamation against learned women.

Elizabeth Elstob (1683-1756)

Do you want employment? Choose it well before you begin, and then pursue it. Do you want amusement? Take the first you meet with that is harmless, and never be attached to any. Are you in a moderate station? Be content, though not affectedly so; be philosophical, but for the most part keep your thoughts to youself.
Are you sleepy? Go to bed.

Elizabeth Carter (1717-1806)

I am not surprised at what George has done, for he was always a very good boy.

>   Mary Washington (1708-1789)

I am well; all is well-well for ever. I see, wherever I turn my eyes, whether I live or die, nothing but victory.

>   Selina Hastings (1707-1791)

If I have learned anything, I owe it neither to precepts or to books, but to a few opportune misfortunes. Perhaps the school of misfortunes is the very best.

Louise Honorine de Choiseul (1734-1801)

I am more and more convinced that man is a dangerous creature.

                    Abigail Adams (1744-1818)

I can not say that I think you are very generous to the ladies, for whilst you are proclaiming peace and good will to men, emancipating all nations, you insist upon retaining an absolute power over wives.

                                  Ibid

This woman is one of those monsters of perfection, who is an angel before her time, and is so entirely resigned to the will of heaven, that she appears to be the most provoking piece of still life one ever had the misfortune to meet.

Sarah Siddons (1755-1831)

Courage! I have shown it for years; think you I shall lose it at the moment when my sufferings are to end?

Marie-Antoinette (1755-1793)

Nothing so like as male and female youth;
Nothing so like as man and woman old.

Anne Douglas Howard (?-1760)

Woman, instead of being elevated by her union with man, which might be expected from an alliance with a superior being, is in reality lowered. She generally loses her individuality, her independent character, her moral being. She becomes absorbed into him, and henceforth is looked at, and acts through the medium of her husband.

Sarah Moore Grimke (1792-1873)

One clear idea is too precious a treasure to lose.

Caroline Gilman (1794-1888)

My dreams were all my own; I accounted for them to nobody; they were my refuge when annoyed—my dearest pleasure when free.

Mary Shelly (1797-1851)

In a world where there is so much to be done, I felt strongly impressed that there must be something for me to do.

Dorthea Dix (1802-1887)

One wastes so much time, one is so prodigal of life, at twenty! Our days of winter count for double. That is the compensation of the old.

George Sand (1804-1876)

As wives and mothers, as sisters and daughters, we are deeply responsible for the influence we have on the human race. We are bound to exert it; we are bound to urge man to cease to do evil, and learn to do well. We are bound to urge them to regain, defend and preserve inviolate the rights of all, especially those whom they have most deeply wronged.

Maria Weston Chapman (1806-1885)

I had crossed the line. I was free; but there was no one to welcome me to the land of freedom. I was a stranger in a strange land; and my home, after all, was down in Maryland; because my father, my mother, my brothers, and sisters, and friends were there. But I was free, and they should be free. I would make a home in the North and bring them there, God helping me.

Harriet Tubman (1815-1913)

To a woman, the consciousness of being well-dressed gives a sense of tranquility which religion fails to bestow.

Helen Olcott Bell (1830-1918)

The Pedigree of Honey
Does not concern the Bee–
A Clover, any time, to him,
Is Aristocracy–

Emily Dickinson (1830 - 1886)

*Woman's mind is as strong as man's -
equal in all things and his superior in some.*

Lucy Webb Hayes (1831-1892)

Sit down and read. Educate yourself for the coming conflicts.

Mother Jones (1830-1930)

They talk about a woman's sphere,
As though it had a limit.
There's not a place in earth or heaven,
There's not a task to mankind given...
Without a woman in it.

Kate Field (1831-1896)

*Woman embroiders man's life-
Embroider is to beautify-
The embroidery of cleanliness-
of a smile - of gentle words.*

Mary Wood Allen (1841-1908)

❦

*From a timid, shy girl I had
become a woman of resolute
character, who could no longer
be frightened by the struggle
with troubles.*

Dostoevsky (1846-1918)

Call no man foe, but never love a stranger.
Build up no plan, nor any star pursue.
Go forth in crowds,
in loneliness is danger.
Thus nothing fate consend,
And nothing fate can do
Shall pierce your peace, my friend.

Stella Benson (1892-1933)

Endurance can be a harsh and bitter root in one's life, bearing poisonous and gloomy fruit, destroying other lives. Endurance is only the beginning. There must be acceptance and the knowledge that sorrow fully accepted brings its own gifts. For there is an alchemy in sorrow. It can be transmuted into wisdom.

Pearl S. Buck (1892-1973)

No matter how loft you are in your department, the responsibility for what your lowliest assistant is doing is yours.

Rowland James (1895-1974)

I stayed busy all the time and loved being in the White House, but I was never expected to do all the things you have to do.

Mamie Doud Eisenhower (1896-1979)

Whatever women do they must do twice as well as men to be thought half as good. Luckily, this is not difficult.

Charlotte Whitton (1896-1975)

My father dealt in stocks and shares and my mother also had a lot of time on her hands.

Hermione Gingold (1897-1987)

I took to photography like a duck to water. I never wanted to do anything else. Excitement about the subject is the voltage which pushes me over the mountain of drudgery necessary to produce the final photograph.

Berenice Abbott (1898-1991)

The women who take husbands not out of love but out of greed, to get their bills paid, to get a fine house and clothes and jewels; the women who marry to get out of a tiresome job, or to get away from disagreeable relatives, or to avoid being called an old maid-these are whores in everything but name. The only difference between them and my girls is that my girls gave a man his money's worth.

Polly Adler (1900-1962)

Money is only money, beans tonight and steak tomorrow. So long as you can look yourself in the eye.

Meridel Le Sueur (1900-1994)

The freer that women become, the freer will men be. Because when you enslave someone-you are enslaved.

Louise Nevelson (1900-1988)

If we are to achieve a richer culture, rich in contrasting values, we must recognize the whole gamut of human potentialities, and so weave a less arbitrary social fabric, one in which each diverse human gift will find fitting place.

Margaret Mead (1901-1978)

I think that to get under the surface and really appreciate the beauty of any country, one has to go there poor.

Grace Moore (1901-1947)

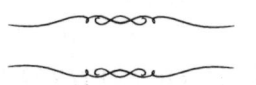

Here's a rule I recommend. Never practice two vices at once.

Tallulah Bankhead (1903-1968)

A woman with a woman's viewpoint is of more value than when she forgets she's a woman and begins to act like a man.

Nelly Ptaschkina (1903-1920)

The inside room was a very private place. She could be in the middle of a house full of people and still feel like she was locked up by herself.

Carson McCullers (1917-1967)

I don't mind the fun and games of being treated like a fragile flower. But as a physiologist working with the unromantic scientific facts of life, I find it hard to delude myself about feminine frailty.

Estelle R. Ramey (born 1917)

Women's liberation is the liberation of the feminine in the man and the masculine in the woman.

Corita Kent (born 1918)

I earn and pay my own way as a great many women do today. Why should unmarried women be discriminated against- unmarried men are not.

Dinah Shore (born 1920)

In the beginning, I wanted to enter what was essentially a man's field. I wanted to prove I could do it. Then I found that when I did as well as the men in the field I got more credit for my work because I am a woman, which seems unfair.

Eugenie Clark (born 1922)

I'd like to get to the point where I can be just as mediocre as a man.

> Juanita Kreps (born 1921)

If hope shows the depth of sorrow, then hopelessness must cure sorrow.

> Eeva-Liisa Manner (born 1921)

One needs something to believe in, something for which one can have whole-hearted enthusiasm. One needs to feel that one's life has meaning, that one is needed in this world.

Hannah Senesh (1921-1944)

Until the time of my own marriage I had sworn I would settle for nothing less than a certain kind of love. However, I had become convinced, after listening to my mother and to others as well, that a union of that sort was too fantastic to exist; nor was it desirable. The reason for its undesirability was never plain. It was one of the definite statements of rejection young persons must learn to make; "Perfect love cannot last" is as good a beginning as any.

Mavis Gallant (born 1922)

Time, dough in a bowl, rose, doubling, tripling in bulk, and I was in the middle of the swelling, yeasty mass—lost.

        Vera Randal (born 1922)

Grab the hope when it flies by, we say.

        Antoinette DeWit (born 1923)

...a sense of deep strain between women and men has been permeating our species' life as far back into time as the study of myth and ritual permits us to trace human feeling.

The Mermaid and the Minotaur (1977)

The dear old ladies whose checks are pink in spite of the years of winter's chill,
Are like the Autumn leaves, I think,
A little crumpled, but lovely still.

Jane Screven Heyward (1923-1939)

A man's illness is his private teritory and no matter how much he loves you and how close you are, you stay an outsider.

Lauren Bacall (born 1924)

..We whose hands have rocked the cradle, are now using our hands to rock the boat...

    Wilma Scott Heide (born 1926)

Great periods of civilizations, however much they may have owed their beginning to the aggressive dominance of the male principle, have always been marked by some sort of rise in the status of women...

    Carolyn Heilbrun (born 1926)

It was hell for women architects then. They didn't want us in school or in the profession. ...One thing I've never understood about this prejudice is that it's so strange in the view of the fact the drive to build has always been in women.

Quoted in *Women at Work*
Gertrued Lemp Kerbis (born 1926)

I have reached the conclusion myself that sex was not a division but a continuum almost, that almost nobody was altogether of one sex or another...

Jan Morris (born 1926)

The Rose Bowl is the only bowl I've ever seen that I didn't have to clean.

Erma Bombeck (born 1927)

You may marry or you may not. In today's world that is no longer the big question for women.

Helen Gurley Brown (born 1921)

I'd much rather be a woman than a man. Women can cry, they can wear cute clothes, and they're first to be rescued off a sinking ship.

Gilda Radner (1946-1989)

...the receptionist is by definition underpaid to lie.

Karen Brodine (born 1947)

This land is the house we have always lived in. The women, their bones are holding up the earth.

Linda Hogan (born 1947)

OTHER CALENDARS BY GREAT QUOTATIONS

Apple A Day
Each Day A New Beginning
Friends Forever
Golf Forever... Work Whenever
Home Is Where The Heart Is
Seasonings
Simple Ways To Say I Love You
To A Very Special Dad
To A Very Special Mom
Teachers are "First Class!"
365 Days Of Life In The Stress Lane
Mrs. Webster's Daily Dictionary
Quotes From Great Women
Baby Boomer's Blues

OTHER BOOKS BY GREAT QUOTATIONS

199 Useful Things to Do With A Politician
201 Best Things Ever Said
A Lifetime of Love
A Light Heart Lives Long
A Teacher Is Better Than Two Books
As a Cat Thinketh
Cheatnotes On Life
Chicken Soup
Dear Mr. President
Don't Deliberate...Litigate
Father Knows Best
For Mother - A Bouquet of Sentiment
Golden Years, Golden Words
Happiness Walks On Busy Feet
Heal The World
Hooked on Golf
Hollywords
I'm Not Over The Hill
In Celebration of Women
Interior Design For Idiots
Life's Simple Pleasures
Money For Nothing, Tips For Free
Motivation Magic
Mrs. Webster's Guide To Business
Mrs. Webster's Dictionary
Parenting 101
Reflections
Romantic Rendezvous
The Sports Page
So Many Ways To Say Thank You
The ABC's of Parenting
The Best Of Friends
The Birthday Astrologer
The Little Book of Spiritual Wisdom
The Secret Language of Men
Things You'll Learn, If You Live Long Enough
Women On Men